NOT UNTIL

'IT'S NOT ABOUT ME'

MARK S FRIEDMAN

Dedicated to
Teresa, my wife,
for her continuous inspiration and support

ACKNOWLEDGMENTS, INSPIRATION, AND DEDICATIONS

Thankful for God's grace,

Teresa, my wife and BFF,

Jeff, who has been my 'iron sharpens iron' for nearly 30 years,

My sons, daughters-in-law, and my grands,

And close pastors, counselors, coaches, and supportive friends.

TABLE OF CONTENTS

CHAPTER 1

STARTING POINT

How far do you have to fall before you realize you have? Fall from your plans...fall from your ethics and morals...fall from your path toward the top of the ladder? How did the motivation and drive to be successful, in everything, every day, suddenly slip through your fingers and completely seem to become just an inaccessible illusion? And, of course, there's the *why*. *'Why did this happen?'* tied with *'How did this happen?'* tied with *'When did I start slipping?'*

Another question I ask myself about falling is: *'How did I get here?'* and *'Didn't anybody seem to notice what was happening?'*

Aren't we surrounded by people who know us, in and out? Isn't it their responsibility (and duty) to monitor our behavior and, like a plane off course, adjust the coordinates and get us back to where we belong? Yes, I know there are LOTS of questions starting off this book, so let's continue. This book is not about me, not solely.

This is a book about us: our struggles, our failures, our challenges.

Who, in your immediate circle of friends and family, is real and honest with you? Is there a 'someone' who feeds you support and accolades even when you are not 'pressing toward' the goals and ambitions you have set in place, defined by your work environment, spiritual walk, or self-conceived dreams (no matter if they are realistic or unrealistic)? And, is patronizing support really what you desire? It may be a confidence builder for the moment, but it holds no real value, and the facade fades rapidly.

How do you define success? Not that definition. Not the one you want to pull out of your last self-help-Christian/business/success/focused/inspirational/company/goal-setting notes. It's realizing that it's not your definition alone...never was and never will be.

I am asking you to seriously take a week to think (yes, a whole week) and define for yourself exactly how you see success, how you spell success, what it feels like, and how it would or how it does impact your every fiber of being. Please do not limit your thinking to business success, as that is not the whole of who and what we (you) are about. Define success as a husband or wife, father or mother, friend, co-worker, son or daughter, uncle or aunt, or son-in-law/daughter-in-law (not in measurement of personal success, but how you positively impact the lives of those who surround you). How about the coach? Include your golf, basketball, or fishing partner, small group leader, or participants. I hope you are now expanding that view you were reflecting through.

I know countless men and women who set off with a vision of what success would look like, only to arrive at a designated point of income, stature, or maybe a title, and the result is an emptiness much like the 'void' or 'incompleteness' experienced when they started. Worse, they (we) arrive at that momentous pinnacle and find more has been lost on the way up—climbing the corporate ladder, chasing the quest for physical achievements, or pushing for that next degree of education—than we ever imagined. In the wake of that focused drive, we leave a trail of devastation and destruction along our path. Relationships...destroyed. Insecurities and fears...actually have expanded. It's not because our choices were necessarily poor ones, but because our intentions were not purposed for something bigger than ourselves. We are the biggest obstacles to our own real success because we rely on our own fortitude, ability, determination, and drive, but seem to forget we have no control over the people and events that interweave and intersect our path. We should dream, drive, pursue, and challenge ourselves toward some definition of success, but maybe we have not quite looked at the 'big picture' as we should. We only seem to see the face in the mirror and not all the faces that are in the reflection behind us.

Every one of us has a different version of what we may describe as our ultimate point of achievement. I would dare to say that there is no such thing, no actual destination to arrive at. Circumstances, educational limits or life changes, physical barriers, and the mix of our individual life experiences are in a constant flux. Those who are involved in and around our lives, along with so many other unexpected and unknown factors, play a part in what that destination may possibly look like at any given moment. It is ever changing, ever redefining; in some part by choice, but in as much by those circumstances we are powerless over. This is exactly what this book will focus on: the journey. We, yes, you and I together, are going to look at the checkpoints in our lives and careers and recalculate our destinations while recalibrating that journey. There is really only a singular journey, but there are countless destinations along the way. I ask you, as we step off into this realm of self-discovery, that you revel in your vast past accomplishments and highlight moments—those that brought great satisfaction and joy. I also ask you to forgive yourself for those moments where you have stumbled and fallen short. Even if you stand, today, in a stagnant, defeated time...well, that's life! Truly, it is. It's beyond your control as to what may come your way, but within your ability to accept, modify, and adapt.

There is no guarantee that we will experience one more week, one more day, or even one more breath. If you are stuck at your previous mountaintop experience and sense only personal failure or inadequacy since that celebratory moment in time, you will miss the many incredible moments that are unfolding before you each and every day. Notice I said *stuck*. It is interesting how we hold on so very tightly to those highlight moments where we have been, as if the past will open up some invisible door and allow us to return. I am sure there are many, many moments in our past that make us grateful that this door does not exist. Imagine having to live through 'that' past experience again!

But back to that incredible moment (or moments) that we retain as a limelight of our existence. It's that trophy moment, that *'it was me'* moment! Since we cannot return, we strive to hit the jackpot once again, stand on the podium of recognition, and secure our one more gold medal. Searching so hard for another 'wow' moment has cheated—and is cheating—you out of possible new, unfolding, and amazing moments, each and every day. Have you wondered, or reflected, on what brought your mind back to that mountaintop? What triggered the need to relive that experience once more?

When you (we) press that rewind button, you find yourself lathered in a wonderful state of gratification and awe. You were *The Man*, or possibly *The Woman*! Everyone wanted to be you. (Well, not really, but it seemed so to you) Can you still 'feel' that elation? Can you? As if you are standing beside yourself, stunned that this was actually you? Wow...and your lips softly speak the words 'that was me' in a most humbling and non-believing kind of way. And as the thought dissipates, it leaves you empty, somewhat longing to experience that, just...once...more.

You can feel that rush! You desire (almost need) to fully re-envision that moment, embellish the emotions...the wonderment that surrounded the attention and recognition that was your stamp in time. It's an individual story for each of us, and although a different story for you, it is also somehow the same, and it will leave you a little...empty.

Often we can get lost in our past and fall into a deep, dark hole of life, or life-lessness... Maybe you are stuck, as I have been, as many coworkers and friends have sadly shared...feet sinking sluggishly into a muddy puddle of depression, despair, or deep lack of self-confidence, being blinded to life's possibilities. That dark place, that awful psychological dogma, is like viewing the most amazing sunset in black and white. The brilliant colors and the breathtaking horizon are there; you just cannot see them. Like that dismal sunset, there is much laid out and constantly unfolding before you, but life has strapped blinders over your senses and emotions, leaving you inadequate to embrace and engage in what is transpiring all around you. There are many factors that can bring you to this awful pinnacle in life: addictions, compulsions, damaging secrets, deep unaddressed wounds in your past, all of which can result in crippling emotional, spiritual, and physical health.

I have walked in your shoes. I have fallen many times. A quote linked to both Gen. Custer and Vince Lambardi goes something like this: *'It is not how often you fall, but how often you get back up.'*

So let's look at that week of reflection you have had (or will have)...

As we begin this segment of the journey, take out a pad and list all the noted accomplishments of your life. It's your list, so base the value of what you have earned on your own bias. ALL of the accomplishments you can think of! It is important that you see your experiences reflected over the many years you have existed and participated in your share of life's timeline. Sometime, during this chapter, ask those who you are close to—like family, business acquaintances, and your friends, past and present—to answer this same question about you. I would not be surprised for you to see that list grow. This is not to somehow falsely accent your self-esteem or cause you to become suddenly prideful; it is to find the balance you will soon desire. Cautiously request positive, noteworthy accolades, as this is not intended to penalize or negatively define you. This is a list reflecting your positive sparks.

As I write, I drift, and I imagine who may be reading this *right now*. The variety of readers, ages, backgrounds, life-styles, economic, demographic, and geographic identities, each sharing their own personal thoughts, as I reflect on my own. Right now, as you are reading and preparing to put this together for yourself, I imagine all of us gathered, seated, at a retreat, in a warm outdoor setting (indoor if it's raining). We openly share our 'colorful bios' with one another as each particular topic in this book unfolds. That's what this is: a reflection of my journey mixed with yours, mixed with those who have shared their stories with me. Our stories all blending together, mixing with all of the faces and names who have impacted and influenced decisions along our life's highway. Every moment, every decision, every landmark in our lives is shared with those who walked alongside, led, or followed us to that pinnacle. Invite them in, one and all, as your thoughts run through past videos of personal experiences.

Who has had the strongest influence on your present character?

_____

_____

_____

_____

_____

_____

Who has had the most positive impact on your current employment?

_____

_____

_____

_____

_____

What would you do for a career if not what you do today? Why? Why aren't you?

_____

_____

_____

_____

_____

_____

What is your biggest regret? Even if you have 'moved past it,' what is it?

_____

_____

_____

_____

_____

_____

Name two milestones in your life. Why do you consider these milestones?

_____

_____

_____

_____

_____

_____

If you could share one item of advice from the archives of your own experience, just one, what would it be?

_____

_____

_____

_____

_____

_____

What is your most dominant personality trait? Don't pretend you don't know.

_____

_____

_____

_____

_____

_____

Is the personality trait above perceived as a positive or negative attribute by others?

_____

_____

_____

_____

_____

_____

Now, ask yourself, 'How does (the above) make me feel?' Write about it.

_____

_____

_____

_____

_____

_____

I am exhausted after that, and I am sure you are, too. I wonder how long it has been since you even thought deeply about some of those moments, and how often you reminisce over some not even listed above. *"I am a slow walker, but I never walk back,"* great words of a great president. These were the words of Abraham Lincoln. However, I wonder what prompts men of greatness to make statements admitting to their vulnerability and mortality. I read several interpretations of this quote and personally feel that he refers to how he spent his time intentionally, evaluating, praying, thinking, and planning, not to simply sit still and do nothing. The idea is not to be in a hurry, not to miss out on the journey.

As we move through life, we should take note, reflect, dream, and think, as we slowly and purposefully continue to move forward toward bettering ourselves. Ok, I really think a lot, and maybe drift a little, as I am prone to envision and imagine. Now, as I write, thoughts race and twist around in my mind, reflecting on so many different facets of my daily life and those who impact my (our) journey. Who comes to mind depends on where your mind is focused. Maybe we envision those who are home with you, your spouse, children, and parents? Co-workers and various staff at work? Maybe you are a student, so perhaps students, teachers, coaches, and office personnel came to mind? How about goals to ride that 100-mile challenge, run that first half marathon, get involved in a hot yoga class, or embrace the challenge of

CrossFit? Do you have socially related ambitions, leading a group, or developing an event? How about your hobbies? And there are those people who make up negative life distractions you pray you could avoid? Whew! Thanks for 'going there' with me.

Even though this is just ink on paper, I can seem like a content puppy, who, suddenly seeing a squirrel in the yard, vanishes in a playful, distracted frenzy... Yes, I can get easily distracted (but pretty much in a good way). ADHD...ADD...whatever it may be, can be interpreted as my strength or weakness, depending on your interpretation. It's one of my attributes, and I will acknowledge and embrace it.

"I am a slow walker, but I never walk back." My desire for us is not to rush through the small black print of these pages, simply to get to the end. There is a final page to this book, but there is no end to each of our actual journeys. So, I challenge you to slowly step alongside me and get reacquainted with yourself. Find who you are and who you would like to be. Maybe, who you would like to be more of. Explore those dreams that sit stagnant in the shadows. *If I can express anything, it is this: know that it is never too late, you are not incapable, and today is a great day to begin!*

CHAPTER 2

SELF FORGIVENESS

Let's begin this chapter with forgiveness...your own. What is it that you are holding on to? What weighs you down and keeps you from freedom? Be honest with yourself, because it is likely a lot more difficult to share that transparency with anyone else, at least right now. Forgiveness can be in the form of allowing yourself freedom from a great failure in your life (although the real failure was not allowing yourself the freedom to fail). Failure is human, a stepping stone to success, the innate gift to humanity following the fall in the Garden. You will fail if you breathe, so free yourself of that pressure and then fall into God's hands. God allows failure for two reasons: one is to realize we are not perfect at anything, ever, and the other is that He is perfect at everything, always.

When we fail, it is an incredible time to renew our humility and ask God for the grace to be ok exactly where we are, at that very moment. It is also the time to realize that what we think is failure (and it may be) is a God moment in our lives. 'Be still,' listen, and realize that God will use this for something we could never have conceived. Oftentimes, He uses those moments to refine us, bring us closer to Him, and give us clarity as to what is most important in life. For me, a portion was a path of education I never walked down, and I allowed that regret to dig into my self-esteem and self-worth. (God doesn't weigh your self-esteem or self-worth based on your level of education or any other worldly levels of achievement). Wait...God moment!

Our falls often begin with a push, either from the outside or inside. It can be depression taking us down, originating from some form of tragedy, or we can be zapped by unforeseen devastation, blindsided by a source of trust. Anger, frustration, fear, and intimidation replace our more desired personas of joy and calmness. Many find substitute outlets to release the screams that are held deep inside, dragging us into additional cycles of self-questioning. We fall over and over and, eventually, may no longer desire to get back up. Destructive behaviors are a result of our response to the building explosions of guilt, shame, and frustration inside ourselves. Sadly, that very behavior can become our new source of guilt and shame, resulting in a seemingly never-ending spiral toward death. Maybe not physical death, but emotional, spiritual, psychological death, as the world goes grey, then black, around us.

How do we get here? How did we get there? We are those who have so often faced defeat and snickered, knowing it was the challenge that drove us! Is that you? The excitement of beating the odds, overcoming an unbeatable opponent, is euphoric, until you doubt yourself. Funny, how the same life situation, played out in a different time and place in our lives, can have such immensely different responses. With time, the plaque builds around our spirit and makes us sad, lonely, or fearful. I know that I do not do fearful very well, so I may become angry or compensate with another distorted emotion to hide my pain. It doesn't work very well. It simply feeds the dark hole in my soul where the plaque is eating away at me.

So, have you identified areas that need forgiveness? Let's do this together, and just so you know, this won't be the last list you compile or the last time you should take the time to let yourself off the hook. You are human, created to be less than perfect and yet sometime along the way, someone planted a seed that told you that you were not good enough unless you were _____.

Come on, fill in that blank. We both know the answer is...*perfect*. And yet here we are, so much less than perfect in the eyes of man and yet so much more than perfect in God's eyes. We are His children, *"For it is God who is working in you, enabling you both to desire and to work out His good purpose. Do everything without grumbling and arguing, so that you may be blameless and pure, children of God who are faultless in a crooked and perverted generation, among whom you shine like stars in the world.* "(Philippians 2:13-15)

Like you, I often seem to see less in me than I was made to be. I focus on my fears and 'amplified' inadequacies, and seem to close my eyes as great opportunities and events pass right before me. So, how is that list coming? Keep thinking, and keep letting go because it is your own, self-created anchor dragging you down through the crystal clear waters where your life could be. It could be, and can be, unless you allow that anchor to drop into lightless depths far, far below, from where it can be almost impossible to return.

Write down each restraining thought and ask God to forgive you. Then forgive yourself. If you feel you brought this to God before (maybe multiple times), then humbly ask Him to forgive you again for doubting that He heard you the first, second, or last time and somehow missed you. Realize He didn't miss anything; you just didn't allow yourself the freedom to let go. Let go! He definitely heard you the first time, so this time, trust Him. With each line you write, breathe deeply and let go. With each painful, life-choking reflection, let go. Feel the fall fading? Feel that sense of peace coming over you? That is the 'peace that transcends all understanding.' Only God can melt away those painful chains that bind us, and He does, because He has a love for us that we cannot fathom. God has given you permission...so let go.

Thoughts to share with God:

_____

_____

_____

_____

_____

_____

CHAPTER 3

PAST SCARS, PAST MEMORIES

When you think about who and what had the most influence on your life, it may seem overall cloudy and non-specific. Maybe it is a question you have not really thought a lot about. Of course, there are many, many small moments, nameless and forgotten people and events, which had some effect on what made you who you are today. This chapter is not to rehash old wounds, those demons you have already faced and dealt with (in one way or another). Think of how you react, respond, withdraw, or attack situations of all types. The simple truth is that we did not orchestrate our foundation in life. We had nothing to do with our early years, geographically, economically, socially...but we have much choice in what we allow to impact us today. Choices to fold or strengthen, choices to move forward from wherever we are, choices to not allow what has weighed us down or stands in our way to defeat us.

It is not surprising that one person comes out of poverty to become a huge financial success, while another struggles, living on the streets, defeated by his or her vision of who they should be. That image is created by where they came from, and they chose not to see the possibilities. Which one are you? How does one person become a dedicated marathon runner, competitive and confident, although they have one or two prosthetic legs and yet the one who is physically capable sits reclined in a chair, comfort food in hand, overweight, and depressed as they reflect on their failures. Unwilling and now unable to find confidence in themselves because of something once said, something once unattained, unhealthy parenting, coaching, teaching, management, but by choice, they have given up.

It is important to listen to healthy criticism. I truly struggle with this one. I am sure someone, sometime, laid a lifelong indentation on my psyche that criticism is bad. So, I am working on this as I realize how helpful it can be to personal growth. It is important to allow those who care to evaluate and help you grow, but if there is nothing positive brought to the table from these sources, it is best to first evaluate their motives and consider replacing them with more suitable candidates.

This may be a good time to reflect on your fears, comparing areas of your life where you are confident and glow with times and occasions when you would prefer to be invisible or absent. Good time to wonder why? How about your personal passions on certain situations or people? What are those things you detest so much that simply hearing related descriptive scenarios makes your palms wet and your breathing unsteady? Ok, maybe it does not provoke that radical a response, but you know where I am going with this.

Unless your fears and anxieties are based on healthy, intellectually sound, and realistic reasons, you are closing the door on your own self-imposed prison cell. For example, having no desire to jump off a cliff strapped to a hang-glider doesn't translate to a personal fear of heights; it's just that you have thought it through, and it is a risk you do not feel equals the experience. Healthy anxiety! (And yes, I would love that experience if you were wondering, but it's not for everyone. Also, it likely will never happen. We are all very different and operate on different levels. This is not to compare you to anyone else. In fact, comparing ourselves to others is extremely damaging and unrealistic. We are not wired the same emotionally, nor constructed equally, physically, or athletically. We are not all thrill seekers, and being passive and reserved is a quality, even a gift, that many intense individuals would pay to experience.

Ready? Another exercise is coming up. Over the course of the next week or so, let's compile this next list. I suggest that you embrace the opinions and input of a spouse, child, or close friend(s).

Fears, Reservations, Aggravations, Joys / Overall life's Bucket list

Ask yourself, what holds me back?

(Joys represent things you really enjoy but do not seem to put time and effort into. Because you hold back on these, list them to reflect on what keeps you distant.)

Fears: _____

_____

_____

_____

_____

_____

Reservations: _____

_____

_____

_____

_____

_____

Aggravations: _____

_____

_____

_____

_____

Joys: _____

_____

_____

_____

_____

_____

Answer this for yourself, and compliment your list with thoughts from those who know you best.

CHAPTER 4

DREAMS AND DESIRES

What do you want to be when you grow up? This was a challenging and dream-inspiring thought when you and I were young boys, (or girls) imagining our future. Seems I always thought of a role where I was a hero, invincible, rugged, fearless, smart, and handsome. I do not ever remember money or accumulation of things being an important part of my daydreams. And then we do grow up, years of mandatory and elective education, mixed with a myriad of life's experiences, dashed with moments of unpredictable wonderment and just as unpredictable devastation.

Being grown-up doesn't feel as different as I expected. Is it? Do you feel like your father, uncle, or grandfather? Are we there yet? Funny thing is, if we had arrived, then what would tomorrow look like? What should tomorrow look like? In fact, what would be the need for tomorrow if we have already reached maturity? I question the whole 'grown-up' concept, since we are forever traveling a road that leads us to unexpected destinations. Maybe maturity is overrated!

If growing up were a road trip, we may start off at 'home.' Imagine your life map and find '*Start.*'

Ok, let's begin.

Next, you would pick where you want to go. When considering your destination, be careful that you don't pick a stopping point, rather than a final arrival spot. If we go all spiritual, then heaven becomes our destination (great and inspirational answer, but good luck drawing that out on a map). As we go through this exercise, I realize that it may be easier to pick highlight attractions and celebrations along the way. Hmmmmm, like graduating high school, college years, job, career, marriage, children, and milestones of our life's unfoldings. Backing up...I forgot those intermediate stop-offs: high school sports and social involvements, church youth camps, relationship, relationship, relationship, first job, second job, third job, career change... Oops, backing up again. Can I, can we, plan out this trip in so much detail?

We control the vehicle, or do we? We control the pace of our journey, or do we? Well, we at least control/ keep the car on the road, or do we? If growing up is still fulfilling dreams and desires, how often do they change, how often must we sit back down with the map and make adjustments for inclement weather that knocked us off course? How about going out of the way several hundred miles, or several years, due to a massive rockslide that permanently altered our course? I don't suggest that we will not somehow reach our grown-up destination, but I do suggest that we are prepared that it looks, tastes, and smells much differently than anticipated. You get a degree in accounting only to process paperwork for a financial firm. Your medical degree and dream of becoming the perfect doctor become a ticket to teaching. Finances fall apart or injuries are beyond recovery, so your professional career just dissipated before your eyes. What now? Pretty sure that stop was not included on the map.

The past couple of months, my personal life has been inundated with sermons and books focused on dreams. Pete Wilson, pastor at Crosspoint Church in Nashville, just finished a series called '*When Pigs Fly.*' This multi-week series took us from recognizing our dreams to actually embracing them and living them out. I won't go further into the series in detail, but I do recommend that you access it online.

Almost in parallel, I was beginning a book by Bruce Wilkinson called '*The Dream Giver.*' A great read, but a very un-traditional approach to presenting a challenging message. It's whimsical storytelling, mixed with excellent, healthy, biblical applications. The book reads like nothing else I have ever picked up, and yes, a good read!

Aside from the books and inspiring messages, my wife and I have spent a lot of intimate time focused on and discussing dreams and what life looks like. In the next chapter, dreams will become a core portion of our discussion. What are the dreams God has for us, for me, for you? Because we do not control very much of our lives, I struggle to step out to embrace those desires. We can empower our destination with planning and excellent preparation; research is at our fingertips to produce a solid, well-conceived schedule toward that success. And, if I am following God's dream for my life, can I fail? Would God allow that? Am I afraid to leave my securities of life to step into a place I know I am drawn to? Is my comfort more important to me than participating in something that could positively change someone's life or lives? Is this my dream or our dream?

In *The Dream Giver for Couples*,' also written by Bruce and co-authored by his wife, Darlene Marie, there is a spotlighted reality that some dreams are for me or for my wife alone. Some dreams are to be shared, and so the commitment and risk become equally shared and, well, possibly, feared. I wonder why we fear to follow God's inspired dreams?

In fact, don't you imagine that even the simplest dreams you have for yourself or your lives are desires that are planted inside you. We should recognize those dreams that stay constant, almost haunt us, and share our excitement and reservations about why they are still dreams and not a reality. Let's pause here and ask ourselves, '*Why not?*' Does your dream involve an investment that you cannot produce? Have you tried...really? Have you sought alternative sources, investors, partners, family, or even government support? My experience tells me that most of us will only push so hard, so far, until we allow defeat to overtake us.

For the most part, and be real with me here, we are comfortable enough where we are in life. After all, it's only a dream. How sad. God does not promise every dream will be fulfilled as we think it will, and that's even more exciting, or crippling, depending on your personality, the scope of the dream, the implications of it's success or failure, and whether you trust God, completely.

Proverbs 3:5-6 says, *"Trust in the Lord with all your heart, and do not rely on your own understanding; think about Him in all your ways and He will guide you on the right paths."*

Some of you are not in a good place with God, maybe don't know Him, or maybe don't believe in Him, so these words do not pierce your heart as they might. However, I do believe that deep inside, you may desire to trust something or someone who can hold your hand and embrace you tightly as you reach for your dreams.

There is another verse that has become words of encouragement and support to my wife and me. These words from a loving, caring, supporting, and forgiving God give me strength and encouragement daily. The verse says, *"For I, Yaweh your God, hold your right hand and say to you: do not fear, I will help you.'* (Isaiah 41:13)

There has to be something bigger than yourself, more dependable than your spouse, brother, sister, or best friend in this life. They are, surprisingly, just like you, struggling at times. They are lost and often ill-equipped to really address your needs and to understand your dreams. They may or may not support you, based on their own interpretation of success or failure mixed with their own fears. This does not mean you would exclude them; on the contrary, having a team to encourage you and...pray for you...is priceless! God placed those individuals in your life for a reason. It's His reason, and one you may never understand and may not reveal itself in your lifetime, but is Godly in wisdom and reason, nonetheless.

God tells us His ways are not our ways. It all comes down to trusting God. It ALWAYS comes down to trust! I was seeking to fill this moment in the book with a real story or two, but as I reflected on the subject, I became overwhelmed with the people who would pour into the scenario. So many as it is likely you and I are two of those stories, today. If we do not reach the goal set by our dreams, our goal as defined by ourselves, we consider it a failure. I now consider it an interpretation. Including ourselves, we can make a lengthy list of those who were once great athletes, stopped short in that lifelong dream due to injury or illness. We could wonder if it was actually the dream God had for us (you, me, them). Obviously, there was a passion, a deep-rooted desire inside. But was that passion driven by vanity and a need for popularity and attention? Does it matter?

I have to say, yes, as God would most assuredly move us away from self when it may be destructive. He does also promise to give us the desires of our hearts, so that may cause you to wrestle with your thoughts a little (I have done so, a lot, so please take some personal time for that one). It will wear you out if you try too hard to figure out God's every thought, plan, and action for your life. Regardless, whether this person's motives were selfish and vain or dreams set inside us, there are many whose athletic pursuits were/are shattered by injury or illness. Why? If God gave us that desire, if that seed is embedded so securely within us, how can He just pull that rug out from under our feet?

I have my own summation on that. We see forever in life, but God sees a season. We want it all; He desires to share a taste. We see dreams crumble, but He sees new opportunities that are set in motion by changing the game plan.

Athletes one and all share, a unique force and strength within each of them, impanted by God. The years of disciplined training and determination will now prepare them for something greater and more rewarding than their previous dream ever conceived. *"He will take them by the right hand and..."* If they trust, if we trust, and fearlessly step forward in pursuit of that dream, a dream only God could completely foresee and slowly reveal, maybe we will never again score a touchdown, but that inner gift from God may bring food to a hungry, struggling inner city.

Maybe crowds will not fill the bleachers, their cheers echoing loudly as your shot pops the net, but the wide-eyed five-year-olds and their dads listen as you teach them the joy of a sport once played...drizzled with a message of hope and grace. Maybe that drive, once the physical competition has slowed, works to raise funds to build wells in Africa, or orphanages in Haiti, delivering hope to a world of hopelessness in some other desperate place on the globe. That dream, the dream of an athlete, creates a person who understands perseverance, adversity, and defeat and yet chooses to rise above. Same dream, different interpretation...but His.

There is no exclusivity to using the profile of an athlete to that of a gifted writer, creative artist or musician, or anyone who is drawn to excellence in any capacity. I only use an analogy that relates most to myself. Even then, I wonder if that drive inside is from the love and desire of a single passion, or is it that we focus that giftedness on just that portion of our being...for a season?

Have you ever shared your dreams with any of those named above: family, friends, close co-workers? Have they shared with you? Want to have some fun? Invite a select few to hang out for a 'share-your-dream session. Talk about the business you've always felt called to get involved in, a mission trip or ministry that you would love to embrace, the education that has eluded you, that book you want to write, backpacking abroad, or joining an archeological team—or maybe your wife's long-held dream.

I bet—well, if I *did* bet—that she will read this and it will rekindle a very strong dream she has held deep inside most of her life. I will also dare to say that she doesn't believe she would, or could, ever experience this. Why? Why do we dismiss our deep longings as if they are not attainable? We use rationalization like 'That's crazy thinking,' or 'Maybe ten years ago,' or '*If I*

_____.

Please fill in your own blank because I am sure you have a library of reasons *why not.* The question is not really '*Why haven't you?*'—or *I*—but '*Why don't we?*'

We are discussing inspired dreams, desires of our hearts that are planted by our Creator, to explore and to participate in a world and in a life He created us for.

So ask yourself, *'What are my dreams?'* In fact, get that group together and begin to explore your dreams and theirs as well. Support and encourage one another to risk failure and trust God.

CHAPTER 5

WHAT EXACTLY IS LOVE

Last night, we attended a wedding. Weddings seem to be difficult arenas for us to visit as they stir emotions and questions of *hows* and *whys*. Even for me, sitting and listening to the vows, I was struck with a new reality. As the two stand before God, their families, and friends, they vow not to do something or many *somethings*. Their promises include faithfulness (of course), commitment, dedication, and unending love. This is all good stuff and honorable, but love is not love until it is tested. We all have the ability to love the lovely, or in other words, to love those who do not bring us conflict, pain, hurt, or disappointment. We can easily love when the people who fall into this category are, well, easy to love.

This next portion deals specifically with those who know and have a relationship with Christ, and here is why: without Christ, we have nothing to fall back on when the person (in the scenario of the wedding) or persons (as in our mom, dad, sister, brother, etc.) fail us. Actually, I do not see people failing each other; they fail themselves... They fail God, and we get caught in the flood waters of depression, despair, unbelief, anger, frustration, doubt, fear, and bitterness. If we remove God from that equation, we are stuck to try and rationalize the trauma on our own, within our own limited scope of understanding. The weight of that challenge may even crush us. In the past few months, I have learned of true love and not from God alone, but how He manifests that love in those around us.

While listening to the vows, I wondered: *When your spouse fails you (not if), what will you do? What will you think then? Have you, on this day, already established a non-forgivable list you hold invisibly over your spouse's head?*

I find it crippling to imagine that we do start our life journey with someone we love but already have set pre-requisites in place to 'control' how satisfying, rewarding and enjoyable our lives together will be by placing restrictions on our love. I am certain God did not do that for us, and to ask us to reflect Christ in how we love others removes that option from a Godly perspective. I would not say it is easy to forgive a spouse who breaks our expectations in any way, be it infidelity, drug abuse, criminal activity, alcohol, or even public humiliation due to some poorly chosen action...and yet we do.

Love is an action you give, not receive. Love is stepping past your own hurt, despair, and darkness and giving healing power to the one you promised to give that love to. I am witness to what that looks like. It is supernatural, as only God can give that kind of strength, that desire to embrace when your mind and emotions are ripped apart.

CHAPTER 6

SETTING OUR OWN STAGE

My wife has a counselor/friend who uses an analogy involving a Rubik's cube. I'm not totally sure how it is used, but it doesn't matter. What matters is how it strangely parallels our lives. As I drove home this evening, I found myself comparing that simple yet frustrating and annoying toy to my life. If you are honest enough, I am pretty sure you will see the comparison to your own life as well.

When it's new, the colors line up neatly, as if this is perfection. Each side is a complete match and represents all things in order, the way it is intended to be. *But is that real life?* We are born, grow up, and mature. During that process the squares on our cube are slid around, bumped out of place, and we see that as life's experiences. Each time we were let down by someone, failed a test in school, didn't make the starting lineup for basketball or the band, with every relationship that broke our hearts, for every imperfect, undesired memory flash that we experienced, the blocks shifted.

How often have you tried to put all the colors back where they belong? I have—until I had a startling reality check... My cube doesn't look like that anymore. My colors are faded, scratched, and chipped. In fact, mine looks like the one lying amidst other obsolete toys in a neighborhood yard sale. It's in the 'take it, it's free' box because, aside from the faded colors and chipped edges, it is missing squares. I am not even sure which color blocks are no longer a part of the larger package, but it's incomplete...damaged, imperfect, and incomplete. We try to get it to look like the way the new cube did, only to find that some things are beyond our control.

As I have read before, life happens, and now, it will never ever look like it did before.

This is a moment when you choose. This is that line-in-the-sand crossroad where you may finally let go. I did. I am broken. Truth is, we all are. Different broken pieces on varying sides of our life's cube, but discolored, chipped, scratched, and unrepairable. Well, it is not within our ability to make this anything of beauty any longer, and for the most part, it has lost its initial functionality, but that doesn't mean it is worthless.

On the contrary, it is more valuable as it is than it was new, as are we. The experiences that we would prefer would never have occurred, those that hurt ourselves and those that we love, and the damage we did to ourselves and to others have made this cube unique and irreplaceable. In God's hands, it is a masterpiece, refined more and more each day.

"Then He laid His hands on her, and instantly she was restored and began to glorify God"

(Luke 13:13).

We are not able to see through God's eyes, forgive with His grace and passion, and understand and love unconditionally as He does, as only God can. When I look in the mirror, I see the years etched in my face. If I look deeply, I can imagine the way the cube once appeared, but I can only imagine. When I close my eyes and search deep within myself, there is that same discoloration and distortion to my emotions and my spirit, not God's spirit, but my personal value system and how I perceive myself.

But God's Word says this to me:

"Therefore, if anyone is in Christ, he is a new creation; old things have passed away, and look, new things have come"

(2 Cor. 5:17).

God does not see the missing blocks, the used-up, value-less objects that lay in the 'not worth anything' box. God sees us redeemed, re-made in brilliant colors.

Today, I choose. Max Lucado wonderfully portrays this concept in '*When God Whispers Your Name.*' He lists daily choices with clear and encouraging definitions. The excerpt begins each major line with 'I choose.'

"I choose love, joy, peace, patience, kindness, goodness, faithfulness, and gentleness. Each choice highlighted with application and action. The Fruits of the Spirit are not just fun ideals for children's songs or to adorn gifts and paintings." Ok, so it's not his personal list, but it is inspiring and motivating to address life in this manner each day. Max lists them out with a beautiful, daily reflection of how we could live and treat one another. Sadly, I do not always allow myself to be patient or find joy or peace in my surroundings. But it is also because I do not choose to apply God's principles. I choose to embrace life and challenge it, but not on my own terms; it's not enough. I was broken, damaged, and made worthless by worldly standards, and yet God finds me priceless and unique, so I will choose to act so. I was lost, hungry, and lonely, and when I asked for a scrap of food, I was offered a robe and a feast. I failed...I fell...I could not...but God *can*, and He *will*.

Tomorrow, find a Rubik's cube. Buy it, take it home, mix up the colors, and then smash it with a good-sized mallet or throw it against a wall. Something like that. Crack it, splinter it, abuse it over and over until it looks like you. The real you...yes, the *real you*. Place that beautiful piece of art on your desk, curio, or shelf somewhere, and each day, remind yourself of how much God loves you. Remind yourself that you are one day joining the King, and we are 'like angels.. sons of God' (Luke 20:36).

I believe we all fail to live as if we are truly royalty. I often don't act or speak any differently than those around me, yet I am truly no more than that broken toy without His touch on my life. Do you relate? Can you find yourself mirrored in that reflective thought? I realize that the cube is just a mental connection, a little silly, but don't miss the point. Live, not as though you are new and untested, perfectly put together; come alive each day because you know who you truly are, and yet, though damaged and imperfect, you will never be offered at any price in a heavenly yard sale. You are priceless. We are priceless.

Imagine today is 'that' day. The day your earthly life comes to an end. Years of experiences, joys, sorrows, accomplishments, and failures. Today is that day, one we either embrace or one that terrifies us. I just left the scene of a funeral. It was a young man with a short life, and his life was unexpectedly ended due to another person's poor choices. This other person was writing the last line of the last chapter in his personal book of life. This last line will define his legacy.

Seems that no matter what we do right or wrong, or how much we succeed and fail, this last line could ultimately define us for all eternity. What will your last line read? If the current chapter is not full of color and joy, filled with friends and family who will mourn your departure with great loss, if God is not excited to see you coming, then sit down and break out your pen. Write the ending to your story on your heart and lift it up to God as an offering to change the last line of the last chapter.

The Bible is full of many great names whose stories needed a better ending, and as they worked to refine each chapter as it neared completion, that last line became memorable and legendary in many instances. Moses said no, not me, but freed a nation. David chose unwisely, tried to cover his tracks with deceit, and hid in fear, but surfaced a man after God's own heart. Abraham, Paul, Elijah, Noah, Peter...and on and on. Read their stories slowly. Find the failed, fearful, reluctant people who God embraced and left with a legacy that looked very different by the last few words.

If you are reading this, then it's not over, not nearly. Hand the pen to God, step back, and allow Him to move your story in a different direction.

The stage is set, your story unfolds before the world, and the crowd goes quiet as the lights go dark. All eyes are center stage as each decade of life unfolds. Good times with family and friends. Sad times and times of hurt. The audience gasps as portions are so painful and unbelievable that they exude shock and disappointment. Cries and boos come from the crowd. Passions run high, but then, there is a sudden twist to the storyline. Lights shift and soften, and the crowd sighs. Tears reflect, illuminating each focused face, sparkling as they drip from each corner of the quiet room.

'And then,' is that last line of the last act of your story and the crowd comes to their feet. Thunderous applause rocks the theater walls. An emotionally explosive ending that no one saw coming halfway through the presentation. The reviews will be stellar! I hold the program in my hands and look down. The credits listed for the creation of this masterpiece are clear: the original story written by you. Co-written, as well as the last chapters rewritten, by God's grace.

Today, I choose:

_____

_____

_____

_____

_____

_____

There is a chapter missing from my book:

_____

_____

_____

_____

_____

_____

If I can leave one legacy behind, I wish it to be:

_____

_____

_____

_____

_____

_____

CHAPTER 7

FINDING PEACE

How often do you begin a day with a smile, a joy in fact, a feeling of euphoria that seems to vanish in a slow-motioned breath? I often find it is not one issue or incident that ripples through a calm and peaceful day, but a cascading of many small, unrelated intrusions that leave me feeling beaten up and discarded on the road side (like road kill)! How do we start off with a smiling, *'I can conquer the world'* grin and fall into a crevice of frustration, anger, and/or despair, wondering when and how we arrived there?

This is the sum of our involvement at home and at work. It is the people we depend on, expect of, and interact with that somehow, unpretentiously, create a situation to which we respond poorly, at best. It is never the situation, but it is our reaction to it. We always have the option to choose our reactions, so it is said, but when does that choice become overwhelming to you? Where is that breaking point in your life, and what triggers it most often, in just 'that specific way'?

You come home from a difficult day at work, retreating from your dominating, unrealistic boss (no fingers pointed if that is you), the co-worker who irritates you with countless distractions and life stories you really do not want to listen to, a major life-changing company transition, corporate buy out, position change, removal of the office coffee machine (ouch)... Well, something rocked your world, and without even realizing it, you bring it home with you.

Through the door, you enter with this emotional 'edge'; in fact, you are a simmering pot just waiting for anything to up the temperature, and you will explode. Most likely, the 'trigger' is innocent enough, but combined with an already volatile state, you have no more room for compassion or understanding. You explode! Shrapnel flies in all directions, and destruction surrounds you. Casualties of this tragedy are all around you, with tear-filled eyes shaking in anticipation of the next wave of attack.

But you didn't have to. You chose to, even though you had the potential to hold it in. You were not prepared and had not set yourself up to avoid this fall.

Let's reverse this situation and take issues from home to work. Walking in the door of your office on 'edge'. The drive-in seemed more irritating than normal. You can still hear the echoes from the conflict at home before you slammed the door, wondering what broke as you stormed off. You just wanted one thing clean to wear today; was that really too much to ask for? After all, laundry is not your responsibility. Is it? Don't we do enough? And what about the kids this morning? Could they have been any more annoying?

We leave home already boiling, adding to the broth are a few drivers who cut you off or drive too slow,...mix in a dash or two of self-pity, and let it all simmer as you drive 30 minutes alone in your car. This is not a good recipe for business success. The first person who adds anything to the stew could potentially become the final ingredient.

Ask yourself, as I ask myself, *What did they do?*

In fact, what did anyone do? Nothing. They simply did not live up to your expectations.

Where was your love? Where were love, joy, peace, patience, kindness, goodness, faithfulness, gentleness, and self-control? (Galatians 5-22-25)

I am learning that I cannot be God's reflection unless I choose to. I cannot love others until I love myself. I cannot change the world around me to make me happier, but I can accept the world around me without trying to control it. The world was not created by my hands. My wife was not made in my image to please me but was created as a help mate, my equal, and to be loved as the daughter of the King.

My children are gifts. I did not breathe life into them. Each moment with them is to be treasured. And I am a child of the King. I am to inherit an eternal kingdom, and so I should start living a life befitting such an honor. My job may not be perfect, but I can choose to be thankful for what God has provided for me. I am imperfect, working with imperfect people in an imperfect world. Trying to control what I cannot will be devastating to me and those around me. Loving others and being thankful regardless of my circumstances is freeing. Wouldn't you prefer that kind of mental freedom? (Really, there is only one correct answer.)

This book was stalled for several years, actually, and I did not know why until recently. I was writing about disharmony. I wanted to take you on a journey, to journey with you, and to see the sunrise over the darkness.

Unfortunately, I was stuck in that darkness and could see where I needed to be, and who I needed to be, but unable to move forward. Fear of losing loved ones. Fear of embarrassment and shame.

Guilt and failure wrapped their death grip around me and were slowly choking the life out of my very soul. It was the reality that Christ filled almost all of me that now brought me to my knees. Almost is a big word when it comes to eternity. I fell to my knees and asked God, out loud, to do whatever it would take to break me and free me. Whatever, no matter the loss, the cost.

That's a huge prayer. For years, I prayed. Like many of you who hurt, who struggle, who are afraid of being fully known, I prayed for forgiveness. I prayed for healing. I prayed for redemption. I prayed for freedom. The one problem was that I was not willing to let go at all costs. I wanted to retain some control.

God doesn't work that way. He wanted my all, and so I offered it up to him. He broke me. The worst and best day of my life. No secrets consuming me, like a deadly cancer from the inside out. No more guilt or shame as I laid it at His feet. No more, almost. This was the day that Christ filled me, as there were no more areas within me that I was hiding. I have walked with Christ for three decades, saved—but until now, I never allowed Him to be the Lord of my life. My journey, as we discussed, has not ended, but a new chapter has begun. This book could not be completed until there was a turning point of hope.

Like all situations where a bomb is dropped, it is messy, painful, and requires much rebuilding. Know who those people are in your life who can love you as Christ loves you. Who see you more than the sum of your mistakes and failures. Those who will lift you up in prayer, encourage you, and hold you accountable to succeed.

You may wonder about this books' title... I feel the concept reflects in the story of *Two Wolves*. My wife shared the story with me a while back, after I began writing this. I am fascinated by wolves in a way I cannot truly explain, so this flew all over me. It is an old Cherokee Indian story that describes us as having a good wolf and a bad wolf within us, battling.

The story is told by a grandfather to his grandson. One wolf is good; one is evil. The evil one is made of anger, envy, jealousy, sorrow, regret, greed, arrogance, self-pity, guilt, resentment, inferiority, lies, false pride, superiority, and ego. The other wolf is good. I naturally tend to see the good wolf as a white wolf and the evil wolf as dark grey. (I am very visual anyway.) The good wolf is made of joy, peace, hope, love, serenity, humility, kindness, benevolence, empathy, generosity, truth, compassion, and faith.

In the story, the grandson asks which one wins.

I love the answer because it is hauntingly true. The Old Cherokee told his grandson, "The one you feed."

Perhaps it is the Spirit of the Lord representing the good wolf.

I leave you with this thought...

'You can never truly appreciate the strength and power of God until you have none of your own.'

Not until, it's about God, not me. Not until, I surrender what I want vs what He wants of me. Not Until... It's Not About Me.

ABOUT THE AUTHOR

Passionate, creative, thinker, dreamer, and teacher are the best descriptors to describe Mark. He's passionate about his incredible wife of 43 years, his boys and their families, his amazing grandchildren, and all the activities they all share during the year. His mind never rests, developing facilitated programs to assist and challenge others in their growth, whether it be business, life, or a mix of both.